Mini Pies

This edition published in 2011

LOVE FOOD is an imprint of Parragon Books Ltd

Parragon
Queen Street House
4 Queen Street
Bath BA1 1HE, UK

ISBN: 978-1-4454-4446-8

Printed in China

Created and produced by Pene Parker and Becca Spry
Author and Home Economist: Sara Lewis
Photographer: Stephen Conroy

Notes for the reader

This book uses metric, imperial, and US cup measurements. Follow the same units of measurements
throughout; do not mix metric and imperial. All spoon measurements are level: teaspoons are
assumed to be 5 ml, and tablespoons are assumed to be 15 ml. Unless otherwise stated, milk is
assumed to be whole, eggs are large, individual vegetables are medium, and pepper is freshly
ground black pepper.

The times given are an approximate guide only. Preparation times differ according to the
techniques used by different people and the cooking times may also vary from those given.
Optional ingredients, variations, or serving suggestions have not been included in the calculations.

Recipes using raw or very lightly cooked eggs should be avoided by infants, the elderly, pregnant
women, convalescents, and anyone with a chronic illness. Pregnant and breast-feeding women
are advised to avoid eating peanuts and peanut products. People with nut allergies should be aware
that some of the prepared ingredients used in the recipes in this book may contain nuts. Always
check the packaging before use.

Contents

Introduction

These bite-size pies, made with buttery crumbly pastry, will melt in your mouth. There are tiny pies that are ideal for parties and slightly larger pies that are delicious for a dessert. There's something for everyone, from pies made with flaky pastry to crunchy cookie-crumb cups.

Muffin pans

Pans come with 6, 12, and 24 sections. If using a 6- or 12-section pan, you will need to bake 2 or more batches of pies for some of the recipes in this book. Metal pans with a nonstick finish are best, because the metal conducts heat efficiently, producing a crisp crust. Different grades and prices are available. Silicone muffin pans are best reserved for muffins and cakes instead of more fragile pie crusts.

Cookie cutters

You will need a 4-inch/10-cm plain or fluted cookie cutter for the muffin-size pies and a 2½-inch/6-cm cutter for the mini muffin-size pies, plus slightly smaller cutters for the pie tops. If you don't have the right size, check the tops of your glasses, cups, and saucers and cut around these. It is worth buying cookie cutters with edges of different shapes and finishes, including tiny novelty-shape cutters, such as hearts, flowers, stars, letters, and holly leaves.

Cutters for pastry decorations

Make pie lids from flower, heart, or circle shapes stamped out with cookie cutters—use these instead of round lids. You can also stamp out tiny versions of these shapes using mini cookie cutters and stick them to your round pastry lid using milk. If you don't have any cutters, cut leaves freehand with a sharp knife.

Pastry wheel

This looks a little like a scaled-down version of a pizza cutter; buy one with a fluted edge for cutting strips of pastry for lattice-topped pies.

Pastry brushes

Use a clean brush with firmly attached bristles. Ideally, have two in different sizes, one slightly smaller than the other, for glazing and brushing the top edges of the mini muffin-size pies. Wash your brushes after use in warm, soapy water and dry well before storing.

Oven thermometers

Ovens vary greatly in their accuracy, with some convection ovens being very hot. Monitor your oven with a small oven thermometer; they are inexpensive and widely available from suppliers of kitchen wares. Simply hang the thermometer from a shelf so it reads the temperature in the center of your oven.

The importance of chilling pastry

Chilling the pastry after making it enables the dough to relax and so minimizes the chances of it shrinking during cooking. Shrinkage is most obvious when making a single crust pie that is first baked without a filling. Well-chilled pastry is also much easier to roll out.

Baking blind

"Baking blind" means to bake a pie or tart without a filling, and it is done to stop the filling from soaking through the pastry during cooking and producing a pie with a soggy bottom. Soggy pastry not only affects the taste of the pie, but also makes it hard to remove it from the pan. Roll out and line sections of a muffin pan with pastry, then prick the bottom with a fork once or twice and chill again for 15 minutes. Line the pastry with parchment paper a little larger than the pan (crumple the paper up before using to make it easier to fit).

Fill halfway with ceramic pie weights (available from cookware stores), dried beans, or small dried pasta shapes to keep the pastry in shape for muffin-size pie shells. Bake at 375°F/190°C for 10 minutes, then remove the paper and weights and bake for an additional 2–3 minutes, until the shells are crisp and dry. Let the pie weights cool before storing them. Add the filling to the pies and continue to bake as per the recipe. Mini muffin-size pies are so tiny that they don't need baking blind.

How to tell if a pie is baked

Baking times are given as a guide, but it is wise to check on the progress of your pies during baking.
If your oven seems too hot and your pies are browning too quickly, protect the tops with a piece of foil or reduce the temperature slightly. Your pies may look ready on the top, but it is important that the bottom crust is also baked through.

Prepared pastry

While it's great to make your own flaky pastry, sometimes there just isn't the time. Keep a supply of prepared pastry or pie dough in the freezer, or buy it from the refrigerated cabinet in the supermarket.

Lattice pastry decorations

Cut ultrathin or finger-width strips of pastry with a small knife or fluted-edge pastry wheel and either arrange over the pies in 2 layers or interweave different strips for a basketweave effect. Symmetrically arranged strips add form, while randomly arranged strips at converging angles add a more modern twist.

Crimped edges

Decorate the edges of double-crust pies by placing your finger and thumb close together, then drawing the edge of the pastry inward with the blade of a small knife to produce a scalloped edge.

Forked edges

A quick, homey finish can be made by pressing the tines of a fork against the edges of a double-crust pie.

Different toppings

Pies don't have to be topped with pastry; sprinkle with crumble or granola or whirls of soft meringue. Add whipped cream to cooled pies and drizzle with caramel, melted chocolate, honey, or maple syrup.

Egg yolk and water glaze

Beat 1 egg yolk with 1 tablespoon of cold water, then brush this over the tops of the pies using a pastry brush. This produces a burnished golden glaze. Sprinkle with a little sugar before baking, if you like. Traditional cooks used to say that an egg yolk glaze should only be used for savory pies, but you can use it for sweet pies, too, if you like.

Egg white and superfine sugar glaze

This produces a paler-colored finish for sweet pies. (If you don't have superfine sugar, process granulated sugar in a blender or food processor for 1 minute.) Brush the tops with a little egg white, then sprinkle with superfine sugar before baking.

Milk and superfine sugar glaze

This produces a paler finish for sweet pies, not dissimilar to the egg white and sugar glaze above. Brush the tops with a little milk, then sprinkle with superfine sugar before baking. For a caramelized sugar glaze if you are making an open-topped pie, dot the fruit with a little butter and sprinkle with sugar; dust heavily with sifted confectioners' sugar toward the end of cooking and return to the oven for the last 5 minutes, until the sugar has dissolved and caramelized to a deep golden color.

Pie dough for flaky pastry

Makes: 1 lb 6 oz/625 g, or
enough for 12 muffin-
size pies, or 1 quantity

Prep: 25 minutes

heaping 2¾ cups all-purpose
flour, plus extra for dusting

¼ cup superfine sugar,
optional

6 tbsp unsalted butter, chilled
and diced

6 tbsp vegetable shortening,
chilled and diced

4–4½ tbsp cold water

The most versatile, everyday pie dough, this is great for sweet pies. Mix by hand or process in a food processor. The key is to use just enough water to bind the pastry for a wonderful crumbly texture that melts in the mouth.

1. To make by hand, put the flour and sugar in a mixing bowl, then add the butter and shortening. Toss together, then lift the mixture and rub it through your fingers and thumbs. Continue scooping up the mixture and rubbing until it looks like breadcrumbs. Gradually mix in the water with a round-blade knife, then squeeze the mixture together with your hands until it forms a smooth dough.

To make with an electric mixer or food processor, put the flour, sugar, butter, and shortening in a bowl and mix together using the electric mixer, or add to a processor bowl fitted with a plastic or metal blade and mix briefly. It should resemble breadcrumbs. Gradually add the water with the machine running and mix briefly until it just comes together in a ball.

2. Wrap the pie dough in plastic wrap or put it into a small plastic bag, and chill in the refrigerator for 15 minutes. Knead the pie dough lightly on a surface dusted with flour, then roll it out thinly. Using a plain or fluted cookie cutter, stamp out circles 4 inches/10 cm in diameter and use to line a 12-section deep muffin pan. Alternatively, stamp out circles 2½ inches/ 6 cm in diameter and use to line two 12-section mini muffin pans. When you can cut no more circles, squeeze the trimmings into a ball, then reroll this out and cut round lids, strips for lattice tops, or tiny shapes.

Tips

Keep everything as cold as possible. Use butter and vegetable shortening straight from the refrigerator. If your hands feel hot, rinse them in cold water before you begin. Use cold water to bind. A marble pastry board is useful (but not essential) for keeping the pastry cold while rolling out.

Don't add too much liquid. Use just enough to bind the crumbs. For smaller quantities of pie dough, add water using teaspoons, although for larger quantities, you can change to tablespoons. Err on the side of caution; if you use too much water, the pastry will be hard.

Avoid overdusting the work surface with flour. Aim for the lightest of dustings and rub a little flour over the rolling pin. Before turning the pastry, loosen it with a long, flexible palette knife.

Pie dough for all butter pastry

Makes: 1 lb 7 oz/650 g, or enough
for 12 muffin-size pies,
or 1 quantity pie dough

Prep: 25 minutes

heaping 2¾ cups all-purpose
flour, plus extra for dusting

⅔ cup confectioners' sugar

¾ cup unsalted butter, at room
temperature, diced

4 egg yolks

Based on French "pâte sucrée," this pie dough has more sugar than flaky pie dough, is made with all butter, and is bound with egg yolks for richness.

1. To make by hand, spoon the flour onto the work surface, then sprinkle the sugar over the top. Mix together, then make a well in the center and add the butter and yolks. Work the butter and yolks together with the fingers of one hand. Gradually draw in a little flour, working your fingertips in a circular motion but being careful not to let the yolk escape through the flour; use your other hand to flick a little flour around the edges so the yolks stay contained. Blend until almost of the flour has been incorporated, then knead in the last remaining flour until you have a smooth ball.

To make with an electric mixer or food processor, put the sugar and butter in a bowl and mix together using the electric mixer, or add to a processor bowl fitted with a plastic or metal blade and mix briefly. Add the egg yolks and a little of the flour and beat until smooth, then add the remaining flour and mix to make a smooth dough.

2. Wrap in plastic wrap or put into a small plastic bag, chill in the refrigerator for 15 minutes, then roll out and shape as in Step 2 on page 8.

Tips
This pie dough requires careful handling. Always chill it when it is first made, and again when it is shaped. If it is too soft to roll out, roll it out thinly between 2 sheets of parchment paper.

Variations for Flaky pastry and All butter pastry

Cinnamon:	Add 1 teaspoon of ground cinnamon with the sugar.
Chocolate:	Make with 2⅔ cups all-purpose flour and ¼ cup sifted unsweetened cocoa.
Hazelnut:	Toast heaping ⅓ cup hazelnuts until golden. Chop them finely and add with the sugar.
Lemon/Orange:	Add grated rind of 1 lemon or orange with the sugar.

Party Pies

Summer fruit pies

Makes: 24 mini muffin-size pies
Prep: 30 minutes
Cook: 15 minutes

a little butter, for greasing

12 oz/350 g mixed berries, such
as strawberries and raspberries

2 tsp cornstarch

3 tbsp superfine sugar, plus extra
for sprinkling

grated rind of ½ lemon

⅔ quantity flaky pie dough
(see page 8) or 1 lb/450 g
prepared flaky pie dough, chilled

a little all-purpose flour,
for dusting

1 egg yolk mixed with 1 tbsp
water, to glaze

whipped cream, to serve

Celebrate the summer with these gorgeous red fruit pies. The soft berries contrast deliciously with the crisp pastry.

1. Preheat the oven to 350°F/180°C. Lightly grease 2 x 12-section mini muffin pans.

2. Coarsely chop the strawberries and break up large raspberries. Put all the fruit in a mixing bowl and stir in the cornstarch, sugar, and lemon rind.

3. Roll the pie dough out thinly on a lightly floured surface. Using a fluted cookie cutter, stamp out 24 circles, each 2½ inches/6 cm in diameter. Press these gently into the prepared pans, rerolling the trimmings as needed. Reserve some of the trimmings for decoration.

4. Brush the top edges of the pastry shells with a little of the egg glaze, then spoon in the filling.

5. Roll the reserved pie dough out thinly on a lightly floured surface. Cut strips ½ inch/1 cm wide. Arrange 2 strips over each pie, pressing the edges together well to seal, then use a cookie cutter to cut small stars and arrange these over the strips. Brush egg glaze over the pastry and sprinkle with a little sugar.

6. Bake in the preheated oven for 15 minutes, or until golden. Let stand to cool in the pans for 10 minutes, then loosen with a round-blade knife and transfer to a wire rack to cool. Serve warm or cold with whipped cream.

Valentine berry love pies

Makes: 24 mini muffin-size pies
Prep: 30 minutes
Cook: 15 minutes

These dainty pies are delicious while warm. They make a wonderful gift for a loved one. If you don't have a heart-shaped cookie cutter, the heart-shaped lids can easily be hand cut.

a little butter, for greasing

12 oz/350 g strawberries

2 tsp cornstarch

2 tbsp strawberry jelly or jam

grated rind of 2 limes

⅔ quantity all butter pie dough (see page 9) or 1 lb/450 g prepared all butter pie dough, chilled

a little all-purpose flour, for dusting

1 egg yolk mixed with 1 tbsp water, to glaze

a little superfine sugar, for sprinkling

TO SERVE

1 cup heavy cream

grated rind of 2 limes

2 tbsp confectioners' sugar

1. Preheat the oven to 350°F/180°C. Lightly grease 2 x 12-section mini muffin pans.

2. Coarsely chop the strawberries. Put them in a mixing bowl and stir in the cornstarch, jelly, and lime rind.

3. Roll half of the pie dough out thinly on a lightly floured surface. Using a fluted cookie cutter, stamp out 24 circles, each 2½ inches/6 cm in diameter. Press these gently into the prepared pans, rerolling the trimmings as needed.

4. Brush the top edges of the pastry shells with a little of the egg glaze, then spoon in the filling.

5. Roll the reserved pie dough out thinly on a lightly floured surface. Stamp out 24 circles, each 2 inches/5 cm in diameter, rerolling the trimmings as needed. Use a cookie cutter to cut hearts from each circle, some tiny, some bigger. Use the rounds and bigger hearts as lids, pressing the edges together. Brush egg glaze over the pastry and sprinkle with superfine sugar.

6. Bake in the preheated oven for 15 minutes, or until golden. Let stand to cool in the pans for 10 minutes, then loosen with a round-blade knife and transfer to a wire rack to cool. Whip the cream until it forms soft swirls, then fold in half of the lime rind and all of the confectioners' sugar. Sprinkle with the rest of the lime rind. Serve spoonfuls of the cream with the pies.

Deep South cherry pies

Makes: 24 mini muffin-size pies
Prep: 30 minutes
Cook: 15 minutes

These are sure to evoke happy memories of childhood. They're delicious served still hot from the oven with whipped cream or a spoonful of vanilla ice cream.

a little butter, for greasing

2½ cups pitted and halved cherries, plus extra to decorate

2 tsp cornstarch

3 tbsp superfine sugar

1 tsp vanilla extract

½ tsp ground cinnamon

⅔ quantity flaky pie dough (see page 8) or 1 lb/450 g prepared flaky pie dough, chilled

a little all-purpose flour, for dusting

1 egg yolk mixed with 1 tbsp water, to glaze

2 tbsp superfine sugar mixed with a large pinch ground cinnamon, for sprinkling

1. Preheat the oven to 350°F/180°C. Lightly grease 2 x 12-section mini muffin pans.

2. Put the pitted cherries in a mixing bowl and stir in the cornstarch, sugar, vanilla extract, and cinnamon.

3. Roll two-thirds of the pie dough out thinly on a lightly floured surface. Using a fluted cookie cutter, stamp out 24 circles, each 2½ inches/6 cm in diameter. Press these into the prepared pans, rerolling the trimmings as needed.

4. Brush the top edges of the pastry shells with a little of the egg glaze, then spoon in the filling.

5. Roll the reserved pie dough out thinly on a lightly floured surface. Stamp out 24 circles, each 2 inches/5 cm in diameter, rerolling the trimmings as needed. Arrange these on top of the pies, pressing the edges together to seal. Brush some egg glaze over the pastry. Use a cookie cutter to cut tiny hearts and flowers from the remaining pie dough and arrange these on the lids. Brush egg glaze over the decorations.

6. Bake in the preheated oven for 15 minutes, or until golden. Let stand to cool in the pans for 10 minutes, then loosen with a round-blade knife and transfer to a wire rack to cool. Serve warm or cold, sprinkled with the cinnamon mixture, on a plate decorated with extra cherries.

Peach and chocolate meringue pies

Makes: 6 muffin-size pies
Prep: 40 minutes
Cook: 22–25 minutes

What is there not to like? Crisp hazelnut pastry with a slightly tart peach filling that contrasts with a soft cloud of sweet meringue swirled with melted semisweet chocolate. You don't need to add anything, not even cream.

⅓ quantity hazelnut all butter pie dough (see page 8) or 8 oz/225 g prepared all butter pie dough, chilled

a little all-purpose flour, for dusting

2 tbsp butter, plus extra for greasing

2 peaches, peeled if liked, halved, pitted, and diced

1¾ oz/50 g semisweet chocolate, coarsely chopped

2 egg whites

¼ cup superfine sugar

1. Lightly grease a 6-section muffin pan. Roll the pastry out thinly on a lightly floured surface. Using a plain cookie cutter, stamp out 6 circles each 4 inches/10 cm in diameter. Press these gently into the prepared pan, rerolling the trimmings as needed. Prick the bottom of each pastry shell with a fork, then chill in the refrigerator for 15 minutes. Preheat the oven to 375°F/190°C.

2. Line the pastry shells with squares of crumpled parchment paper and pie weights or dried beans (see page 6). Bake in the preheated oven for 10 minutes. Remove the paper and weights and bake the pastry shells for an additional 2–3 minutes, until the bottom of the pastry is crisp and dry.

3. Meanwhile, melt the butter in a small skillet or saucepan, add the peaches, and cook gently for 5 minutes, stirring occasionally, until softened. Spoon the peaches into the pastry shells.

4. Put the chocolate in a heatproof bowl, set over a saucepan of gently simmering water, and heat until melted. Whisk the egg whites in a large, clean mixing bowl until you have stiff, moist-looking peaks, then gradually whisk in the sugar, a teaspoon at a time, for another 1–2 minutes, or until the meringue is thick and glossy. Fold the melted chocolate into the meringue with just a couple of swirls of the spoon to create a marbled effect. Spoon into the pies.

5. Bake in the preheated oven for 5–7 minutes, or until the meringue peaks are golden and just cooked through. Let stand to cool in the pan for 10 minutes, then loosen with a round-blade knife and transfer to a wire rack to cool. Serve warm.

Thanksgiving apple pies

Makes: 24 mini muffin-size pies
Prep: 35 minutes
Cook: 23–25 minutes

These dainty little high-topped pies have been personalized by adding an initial made from a tiny rope of pastry for each of your dinner guests; if you have a set of little alphabet cutters, then you may prefer to use these. If you prefer, bake these pies in advance and freeze when cool, then warm through when needed.

4 cups quartered, cored, peeled, and diced baking apples

2 tbsp butter, plus extra for greasing

¼ cup superfine sugar, plus extra for sprinkling

⅓ cup golden raisins or raisins

grated rind of 1 lemon

3 tbsp bourbon or brandy

1 quantity all butter pie dough (see page 9) or prepared all butter pie dough, chilled

a little all-purpose flour, for dusting

a little milk, to glaze

whipped cream, to serve

1. Preheat the oven to 350°F/180°C. Lightly grease 2 x 12-section mini muffin pans.

2. Put the apples in a medium saucepan with the butter, sugar, golden raisins, and lemon rind. Cook, uncovered, over gentle heat, stirring from time to time, for 8–10 minutes, or until the apples have softened but still hold their shape. Add the bourbon and cook until just bubbling. Keeping it over the heat, flame with a taper or long match, stand well back, and cook for a minute or so, until the flame subsides. Let the mixture cool.

3. Roll half of the pie dough out thinly on a lightly floured surface. Using a fluted cookie cutter, stamp out 24 circles, each 2½ inches/6 cm in diameter. Press these gently into the prepared pans, rerolling the trimmings as needed.

4. Brush the top edges of the pastry shells with milk, then spoon in the filling, mounding it up high in the center.

5. Roll the reserved pie dough out thinly on a lightly floured surface. Stamp out 24 circles, the same size as before, rerolling the trimmings as needed. Arrange these on top of the pies, pressing the edges together well to seal. Brush milk over the pastry.

6. Shape tiny ropes from the remaining pastry into the initials of your dinner guests or family. Press these onto the pie tops, brush with a little extra milk, and sprinkle with sugar.

7. Bake in the preheated oven for 15 minutes, or until golden. Let stand to cool in the pans for 10 minutes, then loosen with a round-blade knife and transfer to a wire rack to cool. Serve warm or cold, sprinkled with a little extra sugar, with spoonfuls of whipped cream.

Hot spiced pumpkin pies

Makes: 24 mini muffin-size pies
Prep: 30 minutes
Cook: 30 minutes

a little butter, for greasing

heaping 2 cups diced pumpkin

4 tbsp lowfat milk

2 eggs

3 tbsp honey

1 tsp ground ginger

¼ tsp ground pumpkin pie spice

½ quantity all butter pie dough
(see page 9) or 11½ oz/325 g
prepared all butter pie dough,
chilled

a little all-purpose flour, for
dusting

a little milk, to glaze

a little superfine sugar, for
sprinkling

These are always popular for Halloween. Serve them as they are or top with a spoonful of whipped cream flavored with a little honey or maple syrup.

1. Preheat the oven to 375°F/190°C. Lightly grease 2 x 12-section mini muffin pans.

2. Put the pumpkin in a steamer, cover, and set over a pan of gently simmering water. Steam for 15 minutes, or until tender. Puree with the milk in a blender or food processor until smooth. Cool slightly, then mix in the eggs, honey, ginger, and pumpkin pie spice.

3. Roll the pie dough out thinly on a lightly floured surface. Using a plain cookie cutter, stamp out 24 circles, each 2½ inches/6 cm in diameter. Press these gently into the pans, rerolling the trimmings as needed. Squeeze any remaining trimmings together and reserve.

4. Brush the top edges of the pastry shells with milk, then spoon in the filling.

5. Roll the remaining pie dough trimmings out thinly on a lightly floured surface. Use a sharp knife to cut tiny leaves and mark on veins. Brush these with milk, arrange them over each pie, and sprinkle with a little sugar.

6. Bake in the preheated oven for 15 minutes, or until the leaves are golden and the filling is just set. Let stand to cool in the pans for 10 minutes, then loosen with a round-blade knife and transfer to a wire rack to cool. Serve warm or cold, sprinkled with a little extra sugar.

Christmas cranberry and orange pies

Makes: 12 mini muffin-size pies
Prep: 30 minutes
Cook: 30 minutes

Cranberries shouldn't be reserved just for sauce to go with the turkey; try them gently poached with star anise for a fragrant filling in an orange-scented pie crust. The secret to cooking cranberries is not to add sugar at first, but instead when the skins have softened. For a festive accompaniment, serve with whipped cream flavored with orange liqueur.

a little butter, for greasing

1¾ cups frozen cranberries

1 tbsp cornstarch

3 tbsp freshly squeezed orange juice

2 star anise

¼ cup superfine sugar, plus extra for sprinkling

⅓ quantity orange flaky pie dough (see pages 8–9) or
8 oz/225 g prepared flaky pie dough, chilled

a little all-purpose flour, for dusting

a little milk, to glaze

1. Preheat the oven to 350°F/180°C. Lightly grease a 12-section mini muffin pan.

2. Put the still-frozen cranberries in a medium saucepan along with the cornstarch and orange juice. Add the star anise and cook, uncovered, over low heat, stirring from time to time, for 5 minutes, or until the cranberries have softened. Add the sugar and cook for an additional 5 minutes, then let stand to cool.

3. Roll the pie dough out thinly on a lightly floured surface. Using a fluted cookie cutter, stamp out 12 circles, each 2½ inches/6 cm in diameter. Press these gently into the prepared pan, rerolling the trimmings as needed. Squeeze any remaining trimmings together and reserve.

4. Brush the top edges of the pastry shells with a little milk. Discard the star anise, then spoon in the filling.

5. Roll the remaining pie dough out thinly on a lightly floured surface. Using a fluted pastry wheel, cut thin strips of pastry. Arrange these over each pie and brush with a little milk. Sprinkle with a little sugar. Bake in the preheated oven for 20 minutes, covering with foil after 10 minutes if the tops are browning too quickly. Let stand to cool in the pan for 10 minutes, then loosen with a round-blade knife and transfer to a wire rack to cool. Serve warm or cold.

Shaker lemon pies

Makes: 24 mini muffin-size pies
Prep: 40 minutes
Cook: 55 minutes

These are traditionally made with thin-skinned Meyer lemons soaked for hours in sugar before baking, but because they can be difficult to find, ordinary lemons have been used here instead. To get around the increased bitterness, two are thinly sliced and poached in a sugar syrup, then mixed with extra grated lemon rind and juice for a tangy filling.

3½ lemons

1¼ cups superfine sugar,
plus extra for sprinkling

4 tbsp water

4½ tbsp butter, plus extra
for greasing

3 eggs

⅔ quantity all butter pie dough
(see page 9) or 1 lb/450 g
prepared all butter pie dough,
chilled

a little all-purpose flour,
for dusting

egg white, to glaze

1. Lightly grease 2 x 12-section mini muffin pans. Thinly slice 2 of the lemons – you need 24 slices. Put them in a medium saucepan with ½ cup of the sugar and the water and stir. Cook, uncovered, over low heat, stirring from time to time, for 30 minutes, or until the slices are soft and translucent and just beginning to lose their color. Using a fork, scoop the slices out of the saucepan, draining off the syrup, and put them on a plate.

2. Preheat the oven to 350°F/180°C. Grate the rind and squeeze the juice from the remaining lemons. Add them to the syrup with the butter and remaining sugar. Heat gently, uncovered, until the butter is just melted.

3. Meanwhile, beat the eggs in a small bowl. Remove the pan from the heat and strain the eggs through a strainer into it, stirring well. Return to the heat and cook very gently for 10 minutes, stirring frequently, or until the mixture has thickened and is preserve-like. Increase the heat, if needed, but keep a watchful eye; if it gets too hot, the eggs will curdle. Let stand to cool.

4. Roll half of the pie dough out thinly on a lightly floured surface. Using a fluted cookie cutter, stamp out 24 circles, each 2½ inches/6 cm in diameter. Press these gently into the prepared pans, rerolling trimmings as needed.

5. Brush the top edges of the pastry shells with a little egg white, then spoon in the filling. Top each with a slice of candied lemon from step 1.

6. Roll the reserved pie dough out thinly on a lightly floured surface. Stamp out 24 circles, each 2 inches/5 cm in diameter, rerolling the trimmings as needed. Press these onto the pie tops, pressing the edges together well.

7. Make 4 small cuts in the top of each pie, brush the pies with egg white, and sprinkle with sugar. Bake in the preheated oven for 15 minutes, or until golden. Let stand to cool in the pans for 10 minutes, then loosen with a round-blade knife and transfer to a wire rack to cool. Serve warm or cold.

Lemon meringue pies

Makes: 12 muffin-size pies
Prep: 30 minutes
Cook: 18–22 minutes

scant ½ cup butter, plus extra
for greasing

2 tbsp light corn syrup

2½ cups crushed graham
crackers

grated rind and juice of 3 lemons

1 cup superfine sugar

⅓ cup cornstarch

3 eggs, separated

*This all-time classic is loved by everyone, with its
sharp, tangy lemon filling topped generously with
piped or spooned meringue. These are made with a
crumb crust.*

1. Preheat the oven to 350°F/180°C. Lightly grease a 12-section muffin pan.

2. Put the butter and syrup in a small saucepan and heat until the butter
has just melted. Take the pan off the heat, stir in the cracker crumbs, then
divide the mixture among the sections of the prepared pan. Press it firmly
over the bottom and sides of the pan with the back of a teaspoon.

3. Line the crumb shells with parchment paper and pie weights or
dried beans, then bake them in the preheated oven for 8–10 minutes,
or until slightly darker in color. Let stand to cool and harden in the
pan for 10–15 minutes. Remove the paper and weights.

4. Put the lemon rind in a second, slightly larger saucepan. Make the juice
up to 2 cups with cold water, then add this liquid to the rind and bring just
to a boil. In a mixing bowl, stir ¼ cup of the sugar, the cornstarch, and egg
yolks together until a thick paste has formed, then gradually stir in the
boiling lemon juice until smooth.

5. Pour the liquid back into the saucepan and cook over medium heat,
stirring continuously, for a few minutes, until it is very thick and smooth.
Spoon the filling into the cracker crumb shells.

6. For the topping, whisk the egg whites in a large, clean mixing bowl
until they form stiff peaks, then gradually whisk in the remaining sugar,
a teaspoon at a time, for another 1–2 minutes, or until the meringue
is thick and glossy. Spoon or pipe the meringue on top of the pies.

7. Bake in the preheated oven for 10–12 minutes, or until the meringue
peaks are golden and just cooked through. Let stand to cool and firm
up in the pan, then loosen with a round-blade knife and transfer to a plate.

S'more pies

Makes: 12 mini muffin-size pies
Prep: 20 minutes
Cook: 9-10 minutes

This summer camp favorite gets the grown-up treatment: mini crumb shells flavored with peanut butter, then filled with a rich chocolate cream and piled high with tiny marshmallows. They are great with coffee or hot chocolate at the end of a barbecue.

3 tbsp butter, plus extra
for greasing

1 tbsp chunky peanut butter

¾ cup crushed graham crackers
or plain cookies

3½ oz/100 g semisweet
chocolate, coarsely chopped

1 tbsp confectioners' sugar

6 tbsp heavy cream

¾ cup miniature marshmallows

1. Preheat the oven to 350°F/180°C. Grease a 12-section mini muffin pan.

2. Put the butter in a small saucepan. Gently heat, uncovered, until it has melted. Take the saucepan off the heat and stir in the peanut butter, then the cracker crumbs. Divide among the sections of the prepared pan. Press it firmly over the bottom and sides of the pan with the back of a teaspoon.

3. Bake in the preheated oven for 6 minutes, or until slightly darker in color. Reshape the center, if needed, with the back of a spoon. Let stand to cool and harden in the pan for 10–15 minutes.

4. Meanwhile, put the chocolate in a heatproof bowl, set the bowl over a saucepan of gently simmering water, and heat until melted. Add the sugar and gradually stir in the cream until smooth. Preheat the broiler to medium.

5. Spoon the filling into the shells. Sprinkle the mini marshmallows over the top and press them lightly into the chocolate so they don't roll off.

6. Broil for 3–4 minutes, or until the marshmallows have softened and are just beginning to color. Let stand to cool in the pan for 30 minutes, then loosen with a round-blade knife and carefully lift out of the pan. Serve.

Tiny Tartlets

Blueberry tarts

Makes: 24 mini muffin-size pies
Prep: 25 minutes
Cook: 17–18 minutes

2 cups blueberries

2 tsp cornstarch

¼ cup superfine sugar

4 tsp water

scant ½ cup all-purpose flour,
plus extra for dusting

grated rind of 1 lemon

3 tbsp butter, diced, plus extra
for greasing

½ quantity all butter pie dough
(see page 9) or 11½ oz/325 g
prepared all butter pie dough,
chilled

*Crisp, dainty pies with a moist blueberry filling
and a buttery crumble top. Serve while still warm,
with good vanilla ice cream.*

1. Preheat the oven to 375°F/190°C. Lightly grease 2 x 12-section mini
muffin pans.

2. Put half of the blueberries in a small saucepan with the cornstarch,
half of the superfine sugar, and the water. Cook, uncovered, over medium
heat, stirring continuously, for 2–3 minutes, or until the juices begin
to run and the sauce thickens. Take the pan off the heat and add the
remaining blueberries.

3. For the streusel, put the flour, lemon rind, butter, and remaining sugar
in a medium mixing bowl. Toss together, then lift the mixture and rub
it through your fingers and thumbs until it looks like fine breadcrumbs.

4. Roll the pie dough out thinly on a lightly floured surface. Using a fluted
cookie cutter, stamp out 24 circles each 2½ inches/6 cm in diameter.
Press these into the prepared pans, rerolling the trimmings as needed.
Spoon the blueberry filling into the pastry shells, then sprinkle the tops
of the tarts with the streusel mixture.

5. Bake in the preheated oven for 15 minutes, or until the topping is pale
gold. Let stand to cool in the pans for 10 minutes, then loosen with
a round-blade knife and transfer to a wire rack to cool.

Orchard tarts

Makes: 6 muffin-size pies
Prep: 45 minutes
Cook: 32–33 minutes

Apple pies with a twist — they are sprinkled with homemade granola (a mix of oats, seeds, and nuts). Mix and match the topping ingredients to suit your pantry; try barley flakes, slivered almonds, chopped macadamia nuts, or pumpkin seeds.

a little butter, for greasing

⅓ quantity all butter pie dough (see page 9) or 8 oz/225 g prepared all butter pie dough, chilled

a little all-purpose flour, for dusting

1 cup quartered, cored, peeled, and diced pear

1⅓ cups quartered, cored, peeled, and diced baking apple

3 ripe red plums, halved, pitted, and diced

2 tbsp superfine sugar

1 tbsp water

1 tbsp sunflower oil

1 tbsp honey

¼ cup rolled oats

1 tbsp sesame seeds

2 tbsp sunflower seeds

2 tbsp pumpkin seeds

2 tbsp coarsely chopped hazelnuts

1. Lightly grease a 6-section muffin pan. Roll the pie dough out thinly on a lightly floured surface. Using a plain cookie cutter, stamp out 6 circles each 4 inches/10 cm in diameter. Press these gently into the prepared pan, rerolling the trimmings as needed. Prick the bottom of each with a fork, then chill in the refrigerator for 15 minutes. Preheat the oven to 375°F/190°C.

2. Line the pastry shells with squares of crumpled parchment paper and pie weights or dried beans (see page 6). Bake in the preheated oven for 10 minutes. Remove the paper and weights and bake the pastry shells for an additional 2–3 minutes, or until the bottom of the pastry is crisp and dry. Turn the oven down to 350°F/180°C.

3. Put all the fruit, sugar, and water in a medium saucepan. Cover and cook over gentle heat, stirring, for 5 minutes, or until the fruit has just softened. Meanwhile, for the granola, warm the oil and honey in a skillet. Stir in the oats, seeds, and hazelnuts and set aside. Spoon the fruit into the pastry shells, then sprinkle the granola on top.

4. Bake in the preheated oven for 20 minutes, covering with foil after 10 minutes if the granola is browning too quickly. Let stand to cool in the pan for 10 minutes, then loosen with a round-blade knife and transfer to a wire rack to cool. Serve warm.

Caramelized apple tarts

Makes: 12 muffin-size pies
Prep: 45 minutes
Cook: 32–36 minutes

These French-inspired tarts are filled with a tangy apple and lemon custard, then topped with wafer-thin sliced apples and glazed with confectioners' sugar. They can be difficult to remove from the pan because the sugar glaze makes them sticky, so be extra careful.

⅔ quantity flaky pie dough (see page 8) or 1 lb/450 g prepared sweet pie dough, chilled

a little all-purpose flour, for dusting

5 Granny Smith apples, quartered, cored, and peeled

scant ½ cup superfine sugar

finely grated rind and juice of 1 lemon

2 eggs

1 tbsp butter, plus extra for greasing

3 tbsp confectioners' sugar, sifted

1. Lightly grease a 12-section muffin pan. Roll the pie dough out thinly on a lightly floured surface. Using a plain cookie cutter, stamp out 12 circles, each 4 inches/10 cm in diameter. Press these gently into the prepared pan, rerolling the trimmings as needed. Prick the bottom of each with a fork, then chill in the refrigerator for 15 minutes. Preheat the oven to 375°F/190°C.

2. Line the pastry shells with squares of crumpled parchment paper and pie weights or dried beans (see page 6). Bake in the preheated oven for 10 minutes. Remove the paper and weights and cook the pastry shells for an additional 2–3 minutes, or until the bottom of the pastry is crisp and dry. Turn the oven down to 350°F/180°C.

3. Coarsely grate 8 of the apple quarters into a mixing bowl. Add two-thirds of the superfine sugar, all the lemon rind and juice, and the eggs and whisk together. Spoon the filling into the pastry shells.

4. Thinly slice the remaining apples and arrange them overlapping on top of the pies. Sprinkle with the remaining superfine sugar and then dot the pies with the butter.

5. Bake in the preheated oven for 20–25 minutes, or until the filling is set and the sliced apples are browned around the edges.

6. Dust with the confectioners' sugar and return the pies to the oven for 5 minutes, or until the sugar has caramelized. Let stand to cool in the pan for 15 minutes, then loosen with a round-blade knife and transfer to a wire rack to cool. Serve warm or cold.

Mississippi mud pies

Makes: 6 muffin-size pies
Prep: 30 minutes
Cook: 12–13 minutes

a little butter, for greasing

⅓ quantity chocolate or hazelnut
pie dough (see pages 8–9)
or 8 oz/225 g prepared flaky pie
dough, chilled

a little all-purpose flour,
for dusting

3½ oz/100 g semisweet
chocolate, coarsely chopped

¼ cup confectioners' sugar

½ cup lowfat milk

1 egg

1 cup heavy cream

1 tsp vanilla extract

white and semisweet chocolate
curls, to decorate

A dark, rich, almost trufflelike chocolate layer covered in an even darker, crisp chocolate pastry, then topped with soft swirls of Chantilly cream.

1. Lightly grease a 6-section muffin pan. Roll the pie dough out thinly on a lightly floured surface. Using a plain cookie cutter, stamp out 6 circles each 4 inches/10 cm in diameter. Press these gently into the prepared pan, rerolling the trimmings as needed. Prick the bottom of each with a fork, then chill in the refrigerator for 15 minutes. Preheat the oven to 375°F/190°C.

2. Line the pastry shells with squares of crumpled parchment paper and pie weights or dried beans (see page 6). Bake in the preheated oven for 10 minutes. Remove the paper and weights and bake the pastry shells for an additional 2–3 minutes, or until the bottom of the pastry is crisp and dry.

3. Meanwhile, put the semisweet chocolate in a heatproof bowl, set the bowl over a saucepan of gently simmering water, and heat until melted. Beat 2 tablespoons of the sugar, the milk, and the egg together in a pitcher. Remove the bowl of chocolate from the heat and gradually stir in the milk mixture until smooth. Pour the filling into the pastry shells and let stand to cool. Transfer the pies to the refrigerator for 2 hours, or until the filling has set.

4. Whip the cream with the remaining confectioners' sugar and the vanilla until it forms soft folds. Loosen the pastry shells with a round-blade knife and lift them onto a plate. Spoon the cream over the top and decorate with the chocolate curls.

Chocolate and pecan tarts

Makes: 24 mini muffin-size pies
Prep: 25 minutes
Cook: 20 minutes

These tarts freeze well packed into a plastic container. Once defrosted, add a dusting of confectioners' sugar and a drizzle of melted chocolate before serving. Alternatively, warm them in the oven and serve with whipped cream flavored with ground cinnamon or Greek yogurt and honey.

½ cup light corn syrup

⅓ cup light brown sugar

2 tbsp butter, plus extra
for greasing

3½ oz/100 g semisweet
chocolate, coarsely chopped

½ quantity all butter cinnamon
pie dough (see page 9)
or 11½ oz/325 g prepared
all butter pie dough, chilled

a little all-purpose flour,
for dusting

1 egg, beaten

1 egg yolk

scant 1 cup pecans

1. Preheat the oven to 350°F/180°C. Lightly grease 2 x 12-section mini muffin pans.

2. Put the syrup, sugar, and butter in a small saucepan. Heat gently, uncovered, stirring from time to time, until the butter has just melted. Add half the chocolate and then stir until it too has melted. Let stand to cool slightly.

3. Roll the pie dough out thinly on a lightly floured surface. Using a fluted cookie cutter, stamp out 24 circles each 2½ inches/6 cm in diameter. Press these gently into the prepared pans, rerolling the trimmings as needed.

4. Stir the egg and egg yolk into the cooled chocolate mixture until smooth, then spoon this filling into the pastry shells. Decorate the top of each pie with 2 pecans.

5. Bake in the preheated oven for 20 minutes, or until the filling has set, covering with foil after 10 minutes if the nuts are browning too quickly. Let stand to cool in the pans for 10 minutes, then loosen with a round-blade knife and transfer to a wire rack to cool.

6. For the decoration, put the remaining chocolate in a heatproof bowl, set the bowl over a saucepan of gently simmering water, and heat until melted. Spoon the chocolate into a paper pastry bag, snip off the tip, and pipe zigzag lines of melted chocolate over the pies, or drizzle the chocolate from a teaspoon. Let the pies stand to set for 10 minutes, then arrange on a serving plate.

Pistachio and almond tarts

Makes: 12 mini muffin-size pies
Prep: 20 minutes
Cook: 15 minutes

A true French frangipane is made with just almonds, but a mixture of pretty green-tinged, sliced pistachios and ground and slivered almonds makes these luxurious mini pies.

⅓ quantity flaky pie dough
(see page 8) or 8 oz/225 g
prepared flaky pie dough, chilled

a little all-purpose flour,
for dusting

3½ tbsp butter, softened,
plus extra for greasing

¼ cup superfine sugar

1 egg yolk

½ cup ground almonds

a few drops of almond extract
or orange flower water

1½ tbsp slivered almonds

1 tbsp pistachio nuts, thinly sliced

a little confectioners' sugar,
sifted, to decorate

1. Lightly grease a 12-section mini muffin pan. Preheat the oven to 350°F/180°C.

2. Roll the pie dough out thinly on a lightly floured surface. Using a fluted cookie cutter, stamp out 12 circles each 2½ inches/6 cm in diameter. Press these gently into the prepared pan, rerolling the trimmings as needed.

3. Meanwhile, put the butter and superfine sugar in a mixing bowl and beat together until light and fluffy. Beat in the egg yolk, then the ground almonds. Flavor with a little almond extract or orange flower water.

4. Spoon the frangipane into the pastry shells.

5. Sprinkle the slivered almonds and sliced pistachios over the top and press them lightly into the filling.

6. Bake in the preheated oven for 15 minutes, or until the almonds are golden. Let stand to cool in the pan for 10 minutes, then loosen with a round-blade knife and transfer to a wire rack to cool. Serve warm or cold, dusted with sifted confectioners' sugar.

Coffee tarts

Makes: 12 muffin-size pies
Prep: 40 minutes
Cook: 27-33 minutes

Dark, rich, and not overly sweet. Bite through a crisp, buttery pastry shell to a coffee and semi-sweet chocolate custard topped with whipped cream that is flavored with coffee cream liqueur. Delicious served with a cup of strong black coffee.

a little butter, for greasing

⅔ quantity all butter pie dough (see page 9) or 1 lb/450 g prepared sweet all butter pie dough, chilled

a little all-purpose flour, for dusting

1 cup lowfat milk

4 oz/115 g semisweet chocolate, coarsely chopped

2 tsp instant coffee powder or granules

2 tbsp superfine sugar

2 eggs

2 egg yolks

DECORATION

scant 1 cup heavy cream

2 tbsp confectioners' sugar

2 tbsp coffee cream liqueur

1½ tsp instant coffee dissolved in 1 tsp boiling water

white chocolate curls, to decorate

a dusting of unsweetened cocoa, sifted, to decorate

1. Lightly grease a 12-section muffin pan. Roll the pie dough out thinly on a lightly floured surface. Using a plain cookie cutter, stamp out 12 circles each 4 inches/10 cm in diameter. Press these gently into the prepared pan, rerolling the trimmings as needed. Prick the bottom of each with a fork, then chill for 15 minutes. Preheat the oven to 375°F/190°C.

2. Line the pastry shells with squares of crumpled parchment paper and pie weights or dried beans (see page 6). Bake in the preheated oven for 10 minutes. Remove the paper and weights and bake the pastry shells for an additional 2-3 minutes, or until the bottom of the pastry is crisp. Turn the oven down to 325°F/160°C. Meanwhile, bring the milk just to a boil in a small saucepan. Add the chocolate, coffee, and superfine sugar and let stand, off the heat, until the chocolate has melted.

3. Beat the eggs and yolks in a mixing bowl, then gradually whisk in the warm milk mixture until smooth. Pour the custard into the pastry shells.

4. Bake in the preheated oven for 15-20 minutes, or until just set. Let stand to cool in the pan for 10 minutes, then loosen with a round-blade knife and transfer to a wire rack. Whip the cream in a bowl until it forms soft swirls. Add the sugar, then whisk in the liqueur and coffee until thick. Spoon over the pies, then decorate with white chocolate curls and a dusting of cocoa.

Creamy Classics

Cherry cream pies

Makes: 12 muffin-size pies
Prep: 30 minutes
Cook: 25–30 minutes

These light cheese pies are perfect for a special summer picnic, although you may need to pack them with a little crumpled foil or paper towels to cushion any bangs. Serve with a spoonful of whipped cream flavored with a little sugar and vanilla.

a little butter, for greasing

10½ oz/300 g mascarpone cheese

2 tsp all-purpose flour, plus extra for dusting

scant ½ cup superfine sugar, plus extra for sprinkling

2 eggs

scant ⅔ cup plain yogurt

1 tsp vanilla extract

⅔ quantity all butter pie dough (see page 9) or 1 lb/450 g prepared all butter pie dough, chilled

a little milk, to glaze

36 fresh or canned cherries, pitted and drained well

1. Lightly grease a 12-section muffin pan. Preheat the oven to 350°F/180°C.

2. Spoon the mascarpone cheese into a mixing bowl and add the flour, sugar, eggs, yogurt, and vanilla. Beat with a wooden spoon or an electric handheld whisk until just mixed.

3. Roll the pie dough out thinly on a lightly floured surface. Using a plain cookie cutter, stamp out 12 circles each 4 inches/10 cm in diameter. Press these gently into the prepared pan, rerolling the trimmings as needed and reserving any remaining pastry. Brush the top edges of the pastry shells with some of the milk glaze and spoon in the filling. Add 3 cherries to each pie.

4. Roll the reserved pie dough out thinly on a lightly floured surface. Cut strips about ½-inch/1-cm wide. Arrange 4 strips over each pie to make a lattice, pressing the edges together well to seal, then brush milk over the pastry and sprinkle with a little sugar.

5. Bake in the preheated oven for 25–30 minutes, or until the lattice is golden and the filling is just set. Let stand to cool in the pan for 10 minutes, then loosen with a round-blade knife and transfer to a wire rack to cool. Serve at room temperature.

Key lime pies

Makes: 24 mini muffin-size pies
Prep: 15 minutes
Cook: 6–8 minutes

4 tbsp light corn syrup

5 tbsp butter, plus extra
for greasing

1½ cups crushed graham
crackers

⅔ cup heavy cream

grated rind of 2 limes

7 oz/200 g canned sweetened
condensed milk

4 tbsp freshly squeezed limes
(about 2 limes)

extra lime zest, to decorate

These superspeedy mini pies are filled with a luscious no-bake citrussy cream sweetened with condensed milk. They're great to make with kids.

1. Preheat the oven to 350°F/180°C. Lightly grease 2 x 12-section mini muffin pans.

2. Put the syrup and butter in a small saucepan. Heat gently, uncovered, stirring, until the butter has just melted. Take the saucepan off the heat and stir in the cracker crumbs. Divide the mixture among the sections of the prepared pans. Press it firmly over the bottom and sides of the pans with the back of a teaspoon.

3. Bake in the preheated oven for 6 minutes, or until slightly darker in color. Reshape the center, if needed, with the back of a spoon. Let stand to cool and harden in the pans for 10–15 minutes.

4. Meanwhile, pour the cream into a bowl, add the lime rind, and whisk until it is beginning to thicken. Gradually whisk in the condensed milk, then the lime juice, whisking for another few minutes until it has thickened.

5. Pipe or spoon the lime cream into the pie shells. Chill for 30 minutes, or longer if you have time. Loosen the pies with a round-blade knife and lift them carefully out of the pans. Decorate with lime zest curls.

Lemon and blueberry cheese pies

Makes: 12 muffin-size pies
Prep: 30 minutes
Cook: 23-30 minutes

Portions of cheesecake can be a struggle to wade through; not so with these delicious individual pies. A tangy lemon cheesecake is held in a crisp chocolate crumb crust, then topped with slightly sharp crème fraîche and a blueberry topping. Depending on how many guests you have, or how big their appetites are, any leftover cheese pies can be frozen by wrapping each one in plastic wrap and freezing the blueberry topping in a plastic container.

2 tbsp light corn syrup

scant ½ cup butter, plus extra
for greasing

2½ cups crushed milk chocolate
graham crackers

1¾ cups cream cheese

¾ cup superfine sugar

⅔ cup heavy cream

2 eggs

grated rind and juice of 1 lemon

2¾ cups blueberries

2 tsp cornstarch

4 tbsp water

generous 1 cup crème fraîche
or sour cream

1. Preheat the oven to 350°F/180°C. Lightly grease a 12-section muffin pan.

2. Put the syrup and butter in a small saucepan. Heat gently, uncovered, stirring, until the butter has just melted. Remove the saucepan from the heat and stir in the cracker crumbs. Divide the mixture among the sections of the prepared pan. Press it firmly over the bottom and sides of the pan using the back of a teaspoon.

3. Line the pie shells with parchment paper and pie weights or dried beans, then bake them in the preheated oven for 8-10 minutes, or until slightly darker in color. Let stand to cool and harden in the pan for 10-15 minutes. Remove the paper and weights. Turn the oven down to 300°F/150°C.

4. Put the cream cheese into a mixing bowl. Add ½ cup of the sugar and beat together briefly with an electric mixer. Gradually beat in the cream and then the eggs until smooth. Add the lemon rind, then stir in half of the juice. Spoon the filling into the crumb shells.

5. Bake in the preheated oven for 15-20 minutes, or until the filling is just set with a slight wobble to the center. Turn the oven off, open the door slightly, and let the pies cool in the oven.

6. For the topping, put half of the blueberries in a medium saucepan. Add the cornstarch, remaining sugar, and remaining lemon juice, then stir in the water. Cook over low heat until the juice begins to run from the blueberries, then increase the heat and cook until the sauce has thickened. Add the remaining blueberries and cook for an additional 2 minutes. Remove from the heat and let cool.

7. Loosen the pies with a round-blade knife and transfer to a plate. Chill in the refrigerator for several hours. When ready to serve, top each with a spoonful of crème fraîche and a generous spoonful of blueberries.

Christmas candied orange and meringue pies

Makes: 12 mini muffin-size pies
Prep: 35 minutes,
Cook: 15 minutes

Cooking the clementine peel and flesh in a sugar syrup until soft and candied adds an almost marmalade-like sweet tangy flavor to these brown sugar meringue-topped pies.

a little butter, for greasing

⅓ quantity flaky pie dough
(see page 8) or 8 oz/225 g
prepared flaky pie dough, chilled

a little all-purpose flour,
for dusting

2 clementines or 1 small
thin-skinned orange

scant ½ cup superfine sugar

⅔ cup water

heaping 1 cup diced plumped
dried apricots

2 egg whites

2 tbsp light brown sugar

orange rind curls, to decorate

1. Lightly grease a 12-section mini muffin pan. Preheat the oven to 350°F/180°C.

2. Roll the pie dough out thinly on a lightly floured surface. Using a fluted cookie cutter, stamp out 12 circles each 2½ inches/6 cm in diameter. Press these gently into the prepared pan, rerolling the trimmings as needed. Chill for 15 minutes.

3. Line the pastry shells with squares of crumpled parchment paper and pie weights or dried beans (see page 6). Bake in the preheated oven for 8 minutes. Remove the paper and weights and cook the pastry shells for an additional 2–3 minutes, until the bottom of the pastry is crisp and dry.

4. Meanwhile, peel the clementines and finely chop the rind. Separate the clementine segments, then coarsely chop the flesh. Put the rind, two-thirds of the superfine sugar, and the water in a small saucepan, cover, and simmer gently for 20 minutes. Add the clementine flesh and the apricots and cook for an additional 10 minutes, until soft and the water is driven off.

5. Spoon the orange filling into the pastry shells. Whisk the egg whites in a small, clean mixing bowl until stiff, moist-looking peaks form, then gradually whisk in the remaining superfine sugar and the light brown sugar, a teaspoon at a time, for another 2 minutes, until the meringue is thick and glossy. Spoon or pipe the meringue onto the pies.

6. Bake in the preheated oven for 4–5 minutes, or until the meringue peaks are golden and just cooked through. Let stand to cool in the pan for 10 minutes, then loosen with a round-blade knife and transfer to a wire rack to cool. Serve warm, decorated with orange rind curls.

Maple cream pies with orange

Makes: 12 muffin-size pies
Prep: 45 minutes
Cook: 37–38 minutes

Delicately flavored creamy pies with a hint of maple and orange rind. Delicious served at room temperature, with extra orange segments and a drizzle of maple syrup.

a little butter, for greasing

⅔ quantity all butter pie dough
(see page 9) or 1 lb/450 g
prepared all butter pie dough,
chilled

a little all-purpose flour,
for dusting

1 cup heavy cream

½ cup maple syrup

2 eggs

2 egg yolks

grated rind of 1 orange

TO SERVE

3 oranges, peeled and segmented

3 tbsp maple syrup

1. Lightly grease a 12-section muffin pan. Roll the pie dough out thinly on a lightly floured surface. Using a fluted cookie cutter, stamp out 12 circles, each 4 inches/10 cm in diameter. Press these gently into the prepared pan, rerolling the trimmings as needed. Prick the bottom of each with a fork, then chill in the refrigerator for 15 minutes. Preheat the oven to 375°F/190°C.

2. Line the pastry shells with squares of crumpled parchment paper and pie weights or dried beans (see page 6). Bake in the preheated oven for 10 minutes. Remove the paper and weights and cook the pastry shells for an additional 2–3 minutes, or until the bottom of the pastry is crisp and dry. Turn the oven down to 325°F/160°C.

3. Whisk the cream, syrup, eggs, egg yolks, and most of the orange rind together in a pitcher. Pour this filling into the pastry shells.

4. Bake in the preheated oven for 25 minutes, or until the custard is set. Let stand to cool in the pans for 10 minutes, then loosen with a round-blade knife and transfer to a serving plate.

5. Serve topped with extra orange segments, a sprinkling of the remaining grated orange rind, and a drizzle of maple syrup.

Honey, walnut, and ricotta pies

Makes: 24 mini muffin-size pies
Prep: 45 minutes
Cook: 25 minutes

Made here with a crisp, rich, all butter pie dough, these would also taste great with cinnamon flaky pie dough. The perfect pie for those who don't have a sweet tooth. Undecorated pies will keep in the refrigerator for 2 to 3 days.

a little butter, for greasing

a little olive oil, for greasing

½ quantity all butter pie dough (see page 9) or 11½ oz/325 g prepared all butter pie dough, chilled

a little all-purpose flour, for dusting

1 cup walnut pieces

8 oz/225 g ricotta cheese

2 egg yolks

5 tbsp orange blossom honey

a large pinch of ground cinnamon

heaping ½ cup granulated sugar

1 tbsp water

scant 1 cup Greek yogurt, to serve

1. Lightly grease 2 x 12-section mini muffin pans and oil a baking sheet. Preheat the oven to 350°F/180°C.

2. Roll the pie dough out thinly on a lightly floured surface. Using a fluted cookie cutter, stamp out 24 circles each 2½ inches/6 cm in diameter. Press these gently into the prepared pans, rerolling the trimmings as needed.

3. Lightly toast half of the walnut pieces in a dry nonstick skillet. Let them cool, then coarsely chop them.

4. Lightly whisk the ricotta, egg yolks, 4 tablespoons of the honey, and the cinnamon together in a mixing bowl until just mixed. Stir in the toasted walnuts. Spoon the filling into the pastry shells.

5. Bake in the preheated oven for 20 minutes, or until the filling is golden brown. Let stand in the pan for 10 minutes to cool.

6. Meanwhile, for the praline, put the sugar, remaining 1 tablespoon of honey, and the water into the skillet and heat gently without stirring until the sugar has dissolved. Tilt the pan to mix any remaining grains of sugar into the syrup. Add the remaining walnuts and cook over medium heat, again without stirring, for about 5 minutes, or until the syrup turns a rich golden brown. Keep a watchful eye on the syrup because it will suddenly begin to change color, darkening first around the edges. Tilt the pan to mix, if needed, then quickly pour the praline onto the prepared baking sheet and let cool and harden.

7. Loosen the pies with a round-blade knife and transfer them to a plate. Just before serving, top them with spoonfuls of yogurt. Loosen the praline from the baking sheet with a knife, then break or cut it into thin shards and press pieces of it into the yogurt.

Coconut cream pies

Makes: 12 muffin-size pies
Prep: 40 minutes
Cook: 8–10 minutes

An all-American favorite made with a coconut filling and topped with vanilla cream. Ginger fans could try a little chopped candied preserved ginger in the cream instead of the vanilla flavoring.

2 tbsp light corn syrup

scant ½ cup butter, plus extra
for greasing

2½ cups crushed gingersnaps
or graham crackers

scant 1 cup unsweetened
dried flaked coconut

½ cup boiling water

¼ cup superfine sugar

3 tbsp cornstarch

3 tbsp all-purpose flour

2 egg yolks

1¼ cups milk

grated rind of 1 lime

1¼ cups heavy cream

1 tsp vanilla extract

2 tbsp confectioners' sugar

toasted coconut curls or
dried shredded coconut

1. Preheat the oven to 350°F/180°C. Lightly grease a 12-section muffin pan.

2. Put the syrup and butter in a small saucepan. Heat gently, uncovered, stirring, until the butter has just melted. Remove the saucepan from the heat and stir in the cookie crumbs. Divide the mixture among the sections of the prepared pan. Press it firmly over the bottom and sides of the pan with the back of a teaspoon.

3. Line the crumb shells with parchment paper and pie weights or dried beans, then bake them in the preheated oven for 8–10 minutes, or until slightly darker in color. Let stand to cool and harden in the pan for 10–15 minutes. Remove the paper and weights.

4. Put the coconut into a mixing bowl and pour in the boiling water. Let stand for 10 minutes. Put the superfine sugar, cornstarch, all-purpose flour, and egg yolks in a separate mixing bowl and beat together.

5. Pour the milk into a small saucepan, bring just to a boil, then gradually whisk it into the egg yolk mixture until smooth. Return the milk mixture to the saucepan and cook over medium heat, whisking, until thick. The sauce will suddenly thicken, and as it does, you may find it easier to turn the heat all the way down to low so that you can whisk out any lumps quickly. Stir in the soaked coconut and the lime rind, cover the surface with wetted parchment paper, and let cool.

6. Loosen the pie shells with a round-blade knife and carefully lift out of the pan. Spoon in the coconut filling.

7. Whip the cream until it just forms soft swirls, then fold in the vanilla extract and confectioners' sugar. Spoon this over the tops of the pies, then decorate with coconut curls or dried coconut.

Index